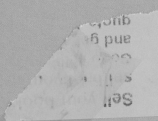

EIGHT DAYS

EDWIDGE DANTICAT

EIGHT DAYS
A STORY OF HAITI

Pictures by
ALIX DELINOIS

SCHOLASTIC INC.

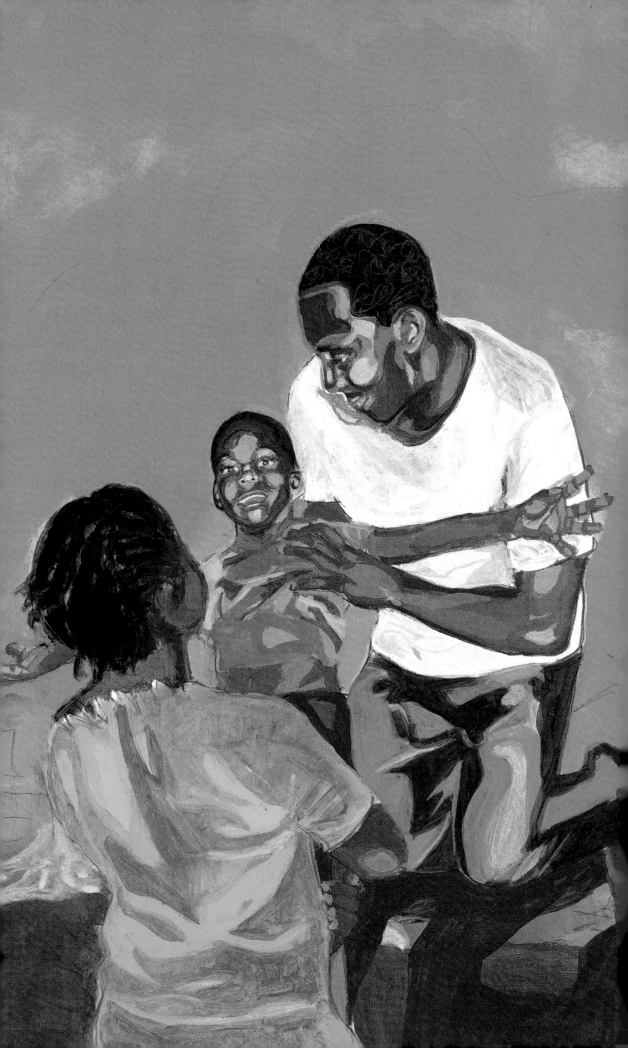

A special thank-you to Matthew McDermott.

Eight Days: A Story of Haiti was originally published by Orchard Books
in hardcover in 2010.

ISBN 978-0-545-64097-8

23 22 21 20   18 19 20/0

Printed in the U.S.A. 40
This edition first printing, June 2013
The artwork was created with acrylic paint, pastel crayons, and collage.
The text was set in 14-point Chaparral Pro Semibold.
Book design by Charles Kreloff and Chelsea Donaldson.

For the children of Haiti

EDWIDGE DANTICAT

*To all living in Haiti. I hope the illustrations
in this book reflect the beauty of Haitian life
before the earthquake, and what is possible
for the future.*

ALIX DELINOIS

WHEN I WAS

pulled from under my house, eight days
after the earthquake, my family was
there waiting.

The following day, everyone asked me,

Were you afraid?

Were you sad?

Did you cry?

I was brave, I told them, but when the
earth shook again and again, I was afraid.
And sometimes I cried, because I missed
Manman and Papa and my little sister,
Justine. But in my mind, I played.

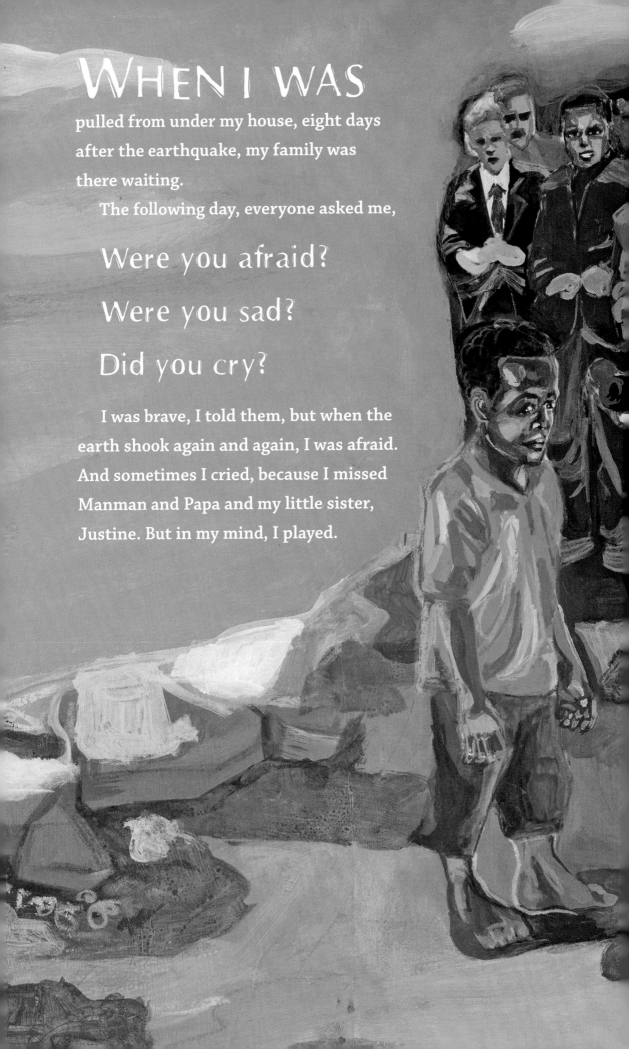

ON THE FIRST DAY,

I flew my kite. And my best friend, Oscar, who was with
me when my house fell, flew his kite, too. It was a windy
day and our kites went high up into the sky.

　　Later, Oscar and I started a game of marbles. We invited
all the kids in our neighborhood to play with us. It was the
biggest game of marbles ever played in our neighborhood,
in the entire country, in the entire world!

ON THE SECOND DAY,

Oscar and I played hide-and-seek. We hid in a dark, dusty corner of the house. And not only did Manman and Justine come looking for us, but Papa did, too. When they came close to finding us, Oscar and I popped up and yelled, *"Alarive!"* Surprise!

ON THE MORNING

of the third day, I teased Justine by pulling her pigtails. She ran into the house, where Manman was using bright red polish on her toenails. Manman made us sit down, and she gave us some paper, and we made paintings with her toenail polish.

In the afternoon, I went to Papa's barbershop and helped him sweep all the hair off the floor, like I usually do.

Then we sat down, and Papa told me stories of the shop and of when he was a boy, like he always does.

Afterward, we went out in the yard behind the barbershop and set the hair on fire. The fire crackled and sparked.

On the Fourth Day,

Justine and I were at rehearsal for the Sainte Trinité children's choir, and I sang too loud. Pè Boyer, our choirmaster, asked, "Junior, are you trying to get that solo again?"

I smiled and sang louder.

And I did get my solo, and it was the best solo ever sung in the church, in the entire country, in the entire world!

On the fifth day,

Oscar and I went out to play soccer with some of our friends. Afterward, we sat on a bench to rest. But then Oscar felt really tired and went to sleep. He never woke up. That was the day I cried.

ON THE SIXTH DAY,

I went to the countryside with my sister, like we do every summer. A warm rain fell and we went outside and jumped in all the puddles. We got soaking wet and muddy. We opened our mouths toward the sky and each caught a mouthful of rain.

ON THE SEVENTH DAY,

Justine and I rode our bicycles around the statue of the conch-
blowing Maroon on Champs de Mars Plaza, across from the
presidential palace. Justine tried to race me, so I slowed down
and let her win.

When we came home, I ate the sweetest mango I've ever eaten. As I kissed Manman, my lips stuck to her cheeks.

Then there was a blackout, so Justine and I recited our lessons to Manman and Papa by candlelight.

Sitting there on the living room floor, I thought about how much I missed Oscar.

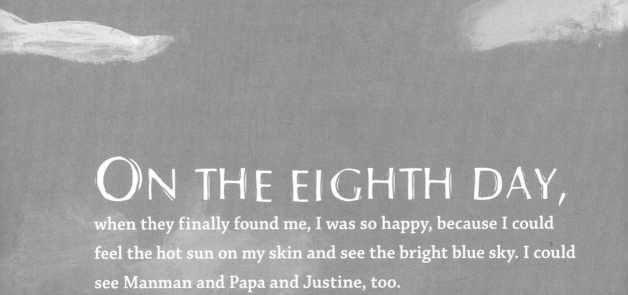

On the eighth day,

when they finally found me, I was so happy, because I could feel the hot sun on my skin and see the bright blue sky. I could see Manman and Papa and Justine, too.

I tell you, I hugged them so tight I thought I would never let go.

A NOTE FROM THE AUTHOR

They are everywhere, Haiti's precious and beautiful children. You see them on rooftops — where there are rooftops — flying kites. You see them gathered in small groups on the ground — where the ground is not muddy — playing marbles. You see them link hands and run in a circle while singing the song associated with the *won*, the Haitian equivalent of ring-around-the-rosy. You see them fight for a turn at jumping rope. You see them twirl a bicycle wheel with a bent rope hanger, and in that act you can see the dream of one day actually driving the rest of the bike, or a motorcycle, a car, or an airplane.

The earthquake on January 12, 2010, dramatically changed their lives. Many watched loved ones die. Others, like Junior, were stuck in the rubble of their homes and were rescued several days later. Yet in spite of everything, Haiti's children still dream. They laugh. They live. They love.

I was at a supermarket in Miami with my two young daughters, Mira and Leila, when a friend called to tell me that there had been an earthquake in Haiti. I immediately began to worry about my friends and family members who live there. Nearly half of Haiti's population is under fifteen, so a lot of the people I was worried about were children.

I was also thinking about children outside of Haiti who were fearful for loved ones. My five-year-old daughter, Mira, for example, was very concerned about her paternal grandmother. "Is Grandma Issa under a house?" she kept asking my husband and me.

Grandma Issa was thankfully okay, but Mira continued to worry about others who might be trapped under their houses. So I carefully told her about a few people, among them some children, who had been miraculously rescued. And in that process this story was born.

When I returned to Haiti after the earthquake, Grandma Issa's Port-au-Prince neighbor, a ninety-four-year old former schoolteacher whom we call Mommy, grabbed both my hands and said, "Thank God your children knew Haiti before all this."

Mira has been to Haiti each of her five years, and her younger sister, Leila, was there the previous Easter when she was three months old. I know they will not remember Haiti the way I remember it, but hopefully Alix Delinois's wonderful paintings (*mèsi*, Alix) will bring some of it back.

I would like to thank Ken Geist, the editor of this book, who called to see how our family was doing the morning after I wrote this story. That call now seems like its own small miracle, and turned what was an extremely dark time into a moment of creation and hope. I would also like to thank my daughters, who remind me every single day that when you look into the eyes of any child, you are looking at much more possibility than words can ever express.

EDWIDGE DANTICAT

EDWIDGE DANTICAT

was born in Port-au Prince, Haiti, and moved to the United States when she was twelve years old. She published her first pieces of literary work just two years later. Edwidge has written many award-winning books for adults, including *Breath, Eyes, Memory*, an Oprah's Book Club selection; *Krik? Krak!* a National Book Award finalist; *The Farming of Bones*, an American Book Award winner; and *Brother, I'm Dying*, a National Book Critics Circle Award winner. She was a 2009 MacArthur Fellow. Edwidge lives with her family in Miami, Florida.

ALIX DELINOIS

was born in Saint Marc, Haiti, and moved to New York with his family at the age of seven. He recently illustrated Walter Dean Myers's stunning biography of Muhammad Ali. Alix is a graduate of the Pratt Institute and has a master's degree in art education from Brooklyn College. He lives and works in New York City.